Strategic Leaders Are Made, Not Born:

The First Five Tools for Escaping the Tactical Tsunami

STRATEGIC LEADERS

ARE MADE, NOT BORN

The First Five Tools
for Escaping the Tactical Tsunami

Rick Mann, PhD

Strategic Leaders Are Made, Not Born:
The First Five Tools for Escaping the Tactical Tsunami.
By Rick Mann, PhD

Published by: ClarionStrategy LLC
www.ClarionStrategy.com

DEDICATION

To an ever-growing number of
strategic leaders
around the world

TABLE OF CONTENTS

Preface   ix

Acknowledgments   xv

Introduction   1
  1. Creating Value   13
  2. Developing Self-Awareness   27
  3. Analyzing Stakeholder Relationships   35
  4. Elevating Your Strategic Altitude   45
  5. Leveraging the Good-to-Great Rubric   53

Conclusion   63

Appendices
  Appendix A: How to Use This Book   65
  Appendix B: Strategic Leadership Assessment   67
  Appendix C: Getting Coaching Help   70
  Appendix D: Recommended Reading   72

References   74

About the Author   77

ClarionToolBox Series

Strategic Leaders Are Made, Not Born – The First Five Tools for Escaping the Tactical Tsunami

Building Strategic Organizations – The First Five Tools of Strategy and Strategic Planning (Coming 2019)

Strategic Finance for Strategic Leaders – The First Five Tools (co-authored with David Tarrant, coming 2020)

Five FIELD Skills for Enterprise-Level Leaders (coming 2020)

The First Five FIELD Skills for Enterprise Leaders (coming 2020)

PREFACE

Welcome to the journey of strategic leadership. Maybe you have been on this journey for decades or perhaps this is all new to you. Regardless, my hope for you is that your experience with this material will be:

- **Clear** – Easy to grasp
- **Concise** – Short and to the point
- **Compelling** – Interesting and profitable

This leadership book is different from many others. I am not trying to address the most common leadership topics. Instead, I am trying to build a foundation of strategic thinking for everyone who is presently leading or those who need or want to lead at a more strategic level.

THIS IS NOT A GREAT LEADERSHIP BOOK

There are some great leadership and strategy books out there. This is not one of them. I am not the most famous leader or thinker and I am not a great writer.

In most ways, this is a foundational work. These are important leadership tools. These are important tools and concepts that every leader should know and be able to put into practice. The first three tools have significant support from the following thought leaders.

- **Creating Value** – The first foundation of business as outlined by Michael Porter and Joan Magretta.
- **Self-Awareness** – Championed by Bill George as the starting point of authentic leadership.
- **Stakeholder Analysis** – John Bryson emphasizes this as pivotal to strategy development.

The remaining two tools, strategic altitude and the good-to-great rubric, are more of my own making.

If you already know these concepts and are putting them into practice, that's wonderful. My hope is that you will share this book with a hundred of your friends who don't know all that you do but instead face their own daily tactical tsunami.

Throughout this book, I will be using a tsunami metaphor. Not only are we reminded of the two most devasting tsunamis to strike in the last 500 years (Southeast Asia, 2004 and Japan, 2011), but this metaphor and the contrasts between these two disasters can help us in our strategic leadership.

USE THIS MATERIAL EVERYWHERE

My goal here is quite ambitious. I want to change your life. These concepts can be applied to your leadership and your organization, but perhaps more importantly, they can be applied everywhere.

Here, I am drawing on Clay Christensen's (2010) McKinsey-award-winning *Harvard Business Review* (HBR) article, "How Will You Measure Your Life?" Christensen is a favorite professor at Harvard Business School and was voted the top management thinker in the world in 2011 and 2013 (Thinkers50, n.d.). He is probably best known for his book *The Innovator's Dilemma* (1997).

Here are a few thoughts paraphrased from his HBR article:

At Harvard Business School, we teach the best and brightest from around the world. We teach them management, statistics, finance, strategy, and so on. Most of them will go into corporate life and have great success. The problem is that many of them will win at work and lose at home. This is a sad tragedy. I wish they could apply what they learn at home first and then in the corporate world.

Again, this is my adaptation of Christensen's words, not his actual words. Not only do I recommend that all of my students read his HBR article, I also have all of my DBA students read his book (2012) by the same title.

With this in mind, I teach all of my students and the leaders that I work with the same thing. My hope is for you to win at life and to win in the marketplace as well. Therefore, I use what I call the PPO approach. PPO stands for:

- Personal
- Professional
- Organizational

Whenever, I introduce a concept, I will offer advice on how you can apply this principle in your personal life, your professional life, and your organizational life. My family will tell you that I have often not done this well. With those lessons learned in my early adult life, I press on in this direction more and more as I get older.

A NOTE TO THE KNOW-IT-ALLS

As I was writing this book, one of my editors showed a draft to her husband who was a business executive. He said that there was not much original work here and wondered what the point was. I agreed with him that much of this material is not original and can be found in other places. I also told him that he was not my primary audience. My primary audience are people who mostly lead and work at the tactical level.

After having taught and trained every level of leader, I have come to see three levels of engagement.

Basic Learners

These are the people who are hearing this or any material for the first time. These learners can sometimes find new material overwhelming regardless of whether it is Chinese or strategy. I tell them to try and grasp the basics. They can make a lot of progress if they learn what they can rather than getting stuck on the details.

Regular Learners

These are learners who can grasp the material with some work and who can go into the deeper nuances of the concepts. With some work, they can also find applications for their lives and leadership.

Know-It-Alls

These are the people who sit out there with a look on their face that implies, "I could teach this better than you do." I say to all of them, "Go for it!" Take these concepts and share them with others who work for you or can learn from you. In the process, they will likely find some places where these ideas could be improved.

THE GOLDEN CIRCLE

The Golden Circle metaphor was made popular by Simon Sinek, the author of *Start with Why* (2009) and the very popular TED Talk on the same material entitled "How Great Leaders Inspire Action" (Sinek, 2009), which, as of 2019, had over 40 million views. Sinek talks about three circles: Why, How, and What. He expounds on why companies do what they do. He then discusses how companies do what they do. Lastly, he talks about what companies do. I have adapted some of his thinking in this work. Each of the five tools listed in this book have the same outline.

WHY It Matters – Here, we look about why the tool is so important to our life and work. This includes the importance of understanding the concepts and putting them into practice. I also include a discussion of why things go poorly when the tool is neglected.

HOW It Works – This is where we unpack the main concepts that are central to this particular tool.

WHAT to Do Next – Here, we suggest what you can do next to put this tool to use in your personal life, your professional life, and your organizational life (PPO).

Enjoy the journey as you and others make your way toward greater strategic leadership.

30 MINUTES PER WEEK

Each tool chapter includes a section at the end that provides practical actions that can be taken in as little as 30 minutes per week.

NOTE: Sources for this book are generally cited and referenced using APA style.

ACKNOWLEDGMENTS

Thanks to all of the strategic leaders who have invested personally and professionally in my life.

I want to thank the hundreds of clients that I have had the privilege of working with over the decades. I have learned so much from each leader and each case.

I can't help but thank the thought leaders who have so shaped my thinking, including Michael Porter, John Kotter, John Bryson, Clay Christensen, Joan Magretta, Bill George and the Carlson School of Management faculty.

I also want to thank the Trevecca Nazarene University leaders who have encouraged me to research, write, consult and coach throughout my faculty tenure. These include Dan Boone, Steve Pusey, Jim Hiatt and Tom Middendorf.

Also, many thanks to my editor, Kara De Carvalho, and my graphic designer, Lieve Maas of Bright Light Graphics, who have been invaluable in the development of this book.

Lastly, I want to thank my family, who have been an ever-present source of encouragement. This includes, first and foremost, my wife, Cheri, who has helped me to become the leader I am today. I am also thankful for our three sons, who are each strategic leaders in their own right.

INTRODUCTION

On Christmas night, 2004, a tsunami hit Southeast Asia, killing over 200,000 people. It struck without warning. In some places, the wave of water reached one hundred feet high. A tsunami occurs when a massive earthquake creates a mountain of water that overwhelms shorelines. The so-called Christmas Tsunami, caused by the third largest recorded earthquake in the last 500 years, left more than one million people homeless and shattered the infrastructure and economy of many communities.

Many days, you may feel like a tsunami has hit you. While not life-threatening, the tsunami of tactical, practical, everyday work can overtake you, your desk and your office with incredible force. Tactical work includes the everyday tasks that fill our days, such as email, meetings, reports and putting out fires in the office.

Tactical work includes the everyday tasks that fill our days, such as email, meetings, reports and putting out fires in the office.

Multitudes of people put in long hours of tactical work every day. Not only can a constant wave of tactical work be exhausting, lots of hard work does not always result in accomplishing your most important goals. Fortunately, it is possible to escape the tactical tsunami and devote more attention to the strategic leadership that is so needed in many organizations. Strategic leaders focus on key outcomes and the strategies they need to achieve those critical results. Almost every professional can learn how to elevate the strategic level of their work and leadership, resulting in greater effectiveness for their personal and professional lives as well as for their organizations.

Strategic leaders focus on key outcomes and the strategies they need to achieve those critical results.

I spent many years, both in China and in the U.S., battling my own on-going tactical tsunami. I put in long hours of work, but I was frequently unsure whether I was making any progress in advancing what I cared about most. All too often, I lacked clarity on how to escape this tsunami and struggled to find the tools I needed to lead more strategically. I was reminded of this one day as I interacted with a VP.

"Stop doing that!" one of my VPs instructed.

"Why?" I asked, startled. I was looking over a mountain of reports from our organization's many directors.

"As President, you have more important things to work on than this," he explained.

I was both upset and embarrassed. On the one hand, I felt like he shouldn't be telling me what to do. On the other hand, I realized that he was right, and that I was not dealing very well with the wave of tactical work. The reports I was reviewing could have been handled well by our VPs without my help. I needed to lead more strategically and give attention to some important areas that only I could address.

This book is designed to help people escape the tactical tsunami so they can devote more attention to strategic issues. The need for this journey is great. Everywhere we look, organizations are experiencing a chronic shortage of strategic leadership that dramatically limits their potential. We can do something about this problem. While the Christmas Tsunami in Southeast Asia was epic in its casualties, a tsunami in Japan tells a different story.

The shortage of strategic leaders dramatically limits the potential of organizations.

STRATEGIC LEADERS ARE MADE NOT BORN

At 2:46 p.m. in Japan on Friday, March 11, 2011, a professor's cell phone rang while he was in the middle of class. Immediately, he instructed his students to get under their desks to avoid falling debris from the impending earthquake. Soon after, his students left the building and sought higher ground before a tsunami hit the shores an hour later. Thanks to Japan's early warning system and that system-generated phone call, his class was able to survive injury-free.

Japan's positive outcomes, in contrast to Southeast Asia, did not happen by chance. The important tools that Japan had put in place made the difference in effecting a 10-fold decrease in the death toll. Equipping people with the right strategic tools can elevate their effectiveness and the results of their organization.

How much time do you spend each month on strategic issues?

Our goal in this book is to give you the tools you need to navigate the tsunamis in your world and to work and lead more strategically. You can make significant progress in just thirty minutes per week, or two hours per month.

"We are going to work on *Death by Meeting*," I said as I passed out Patrick Lencioni's book by that title. I had read the book several months earlier and realized that our senior team spent hours in meetings each week that mixed visionary, strategic, and tactical issues together on the same agenda. We began holding one two-hour strategy review each month. Over time, these meetings were so valuable that we moved them to a half day, calling them our "strategy days." For years, they became our most important meeting of every month and resulted in marked improvements in many areas. Along the way, we conclusively proved that strategic leaders are made, not born, even on our own team. And that was a good thing, since we needed so many more of them across our organization.

WHY IT MATTERS

"How much time do you spend on strategic issues each month?" I asked one of the organization's senior officers.

"We don't spend one minute a month on strategic issues," she replied. "One hundred percent of our time is spent dealing with tactical issues," she added.

At first, I thought she was joking. Then I realized that she was dead serious. How could this be? This was perhaps the most educated senior team I had ever worked with. They had Harvard, Yale and Princeton degrees on their walls. They were a multi-national group with hundreds of employees in over twenty countries. Yet despite their prestigious degrees, they had done nothing to counter the tactical tsunami that was significantly limiting their strategic clarity and ability to reach their most important outcomes.

This organization and so many like it have learned the same lesson as those in the path of the Christmas Tsunami. Tsunamis have no concern for anything or anybody. They sweep away everything and everyone in their path with unparalleled force. Tactical tsunamis function in the same way. They can overwhelm the simplest and the smartest. If we are going to escape these tsunami realities, we must raise up a generation of strategic leaders.

Over the last 25+ years, I have had the privilege of working with many leaders and many organizations. I have heard them repeatedly talk about how difficult it is to escape the reach of the tactical tsunami.

These organizations lack strategic capacity—the ability for large numbers of employees to clearly articulate their purpose, vision, and identity as well as their markets, stakeholders and value propositions. Strategic capacity is also about having the focus and discipline to take just half an hour each week (or a couple of hours each month) to move from tactical issues to strategic issues. Lastly, organizations with strategic capacity consistently and clearly know what value they provide to whom and how they are doing. A lack of strategic capacity is often due to a lack of strategic leadership.

"What do you plan on doing when you come?" the organization's CEO asked me.

"I plan on building the strategic capacity of your senior team," I answered as I looked forward to traveling to their state for a day of meetings.

"We need that for their direct reports as well," the CEO said, adding that this included about 30 people.

"Let's start with your senior team and work down from there." I continued, "Your organization needs strategic leaders at every level."

This organization was very much like many I had worked with. Early on, I thought that a lack of strategic capacity was a product of an organization's small size. However, in recent years, I have worked with an organization that counted over 20,000 employees working in more than a hundred countries that lacked strategic capacity. Recently, I was in Asia talking with a Senior Vice President from Levi/Dockers.

"How are you doing when it comes to raising up strategic leaders?" I asked him.

"Not well," he replied.

I don't have all the answers here, but as a professor of leadership and strategy and as a strategy coach and consultant myself, I have studied this issue now for many years. One thing that I have learned from reading, research, and experience is that most people are tactical and practical in their approach to life, work, and leadership. They are people who work hard and get work done. However, in today's world, simply getting work done is not enough.

Most people are tactical and practical in their
approach to life and work.

HOW IT WORKS

The perfect storm we now face is that in times of great change, even more strategic leadership is required. John Kotter, a professor at Harvard Business School, is an expert in leadership, change and strategy. He is probably best known for his book *Leading Change* (2010), which I recommend to everyone. In an article he wrote for the *Harvard Business Review* (HBR) in 1990, entitled "What Leaders Really Do," he highlights the key differences between leadership and management:

> **Management** is about coping with complexities...**Leadership**, by contrast, is about change. Part of the reason it has become so important in recent years is because the world is more competitive and volatile. Major changes are more and more necessary to survive and compete effectively in this new environment. **More change requires more leadership**. (p. 104)

This could have been written today instead of in 1990. Kotter saw that more leadership was needed as the pace of change quickened. Bob Johansen (2012) uses the acronym "VUCA" to describe our world today: Volatile, Uncertain, Complex, and Ambiguous. To address our VUCA world, in their 2014 book *Becoming a Strategic Leader*, Hughes, Beatty, and Dinwoodie (2014) insist that, "today's strategic leaders must be able to think, act, and influence in that [VUCA] environment." (p. 2)

The job of strategy is not limited to a few top executives.

While the need for strategic leadership has increased as our world has changed, there is also a need for strategic leadership at every level. Kate Beatty (2010) insists:

> The job of strategy is not limited to a few top executives. **Strategic leaders are needed throughout** our organizations if they are to adapt, innovate and succeed well into the future. (para. 10)

Hughes et al. also support this line of thinking, asserting that, "increasingly organizations are calling on people at all levels to be strategic." (2014, Chapter 1, para. 5)

Statistics show that fewer than 10% of leaders exhibit strategic skills.

Lastly, we mentioned above that most workers and leaders are inclined towards doing tactical, practical work. Researchers tell us that most people are not wired for strategic leadership. Beatty (2010) also writes:

> Statistics show that **fewer than 10% of leaders exhibit strategic skills**, a woefully inadequate number considering the demands on organizations today. (para. 1)

Along these lines, Leinwald, Mainardi, and Kleiner (2013) wrote an HBR article entitled "Only 8% of Leaders Are Good at Both Strategy and Execution."

From their article, we can see three reasons for the growing need for strategic leaders:

- More change requires greater strategic leadership.
- We have a growing need for strategic leaders throughout all levels of organizations.
- The percentage of leaders who are well-versed in strategic leadership is small.

Research, evidence, and consulting experience deliver the same message: there is both a growing need for strategic leadership and a low supply of strategic leaders.

You and I have both experienced the tactical tsunami and have a desire to lead strategically. The need is compelling. We will not experience greatness if we live and lead at the tactical level alone. The future of our organizations and the world around us depend on us helping others to lead strategically. This book will give you five tools that you can use to form the foundation for your strategic leadership. I wish that I had written it about 10 years earlier, when I began to notice these issues almost everywhere. Unfortunately, I was doing the same things that many others do. The tactical tsunami in my life and work resulted in me putting off this book for too long.

THE FIRST FIVE TOOLS OVERVIEW

The five tools included in this short book are foundational for every strategic leader. These can help you escape the power of the tactical tsunami and move to the higher ground of strategic leadership.

Creating Value What do you provide that others value?	First and foremost, every endeavor is about being able to create value for others. Creating value happens when you provide a product and/or service that people are willing to pay for. It can also be delivered through financial or non-financial transactions and relationships. Non-financial transactions, such as those found in relationships, nonetheless bring benefits/value to others.
Self-Awareness How are you unique?	Many important measures of success are related to how well we understand ourselves and the experience others have of us. We each have different levels of versatility that allow us to work and lead effectively outside of our natural tendencies in certain situations.
Stakeholder Analysis Whom do you serve?	Life and leadership are not just about you. People want to hire you, work with you, or be in a relationship with you because you consistently bring something they value. Most of us have four to eight important stakeholder groups that have invested in what we are doing in life, work, and leadership.
Strategic Altitude At what altitude do you lead?	While most people are wired to work and lead at the tactical and practical levels, there is a tremendous need today for those who can work and lead at a higher strategic level.
Good-to-Great Rubric Are you getting better?	While it is easy to say that things are fine, there is a greater need for most of us to more finely differentiate between good-to-great work and just adequate work.

WHAT YOU CAN DO NEXT

We are learning that new insights, tools, and practices can move us forward in developing a larger team of strategic leaders. In a similar way concerning tsunamis, over the last 15 years much has been done to develop the International Early Warning Program (IEWP), which quickly alerts of impending earthquakes and tsunamis. These tools put everyone in the world in a better and safer place. In the same way, everyone can develop tools to better understand and engage strategic leadership. With intentionality, equipping, and experience, strategic leaders can be developed at every level.

With intentionality, equipping, and experience, strategic leaders can be developed at every level.

Everywhere we turn, people are overwhelmed by the tactical tsunami of everyday work. Again, tactical work is that on-the-ground, every day, practical stuff that includes the email, calls, meetings, reports, and other routine tasks that overload many of us in today's workplace.

While the majority of people are wired to work and lead on a tactical level, most people can move to the higher ground of greater strategic leadership. By following these three important next steps, your journey toward strategic leadership can be accelerated in as little as 30 minutes each week:

- Gaining strategic leadership **insight.**
- **Practicing** in real world settings.
- **Being coached** by others.

The insights, skills, and practices that you develop can be instrumental in helping you to lead more strategically. This can result in:

- Feeling better about your work.
- Reaching more of your goals.
- Greater clarity as to where you are headed, how you are going to get there, and how you are doing.

These tools have many applications. With each tool, we adopt a PPO approach that will apply the tool to the following three important areas:

- **Personal:** Here, we look at how you can use the tool to create greater value and benefits in relationships with your family and friends.
- **Professional:** We want to grow the value that you can bring to your work settings.
- **Organizational:** We can strengthen the effectiveness of your organization for your markets.

While growing strategic leadership is within almost everyone's reach, most people will not embark on this journey. Many cannot bring the focus and discipline that are needed to move forward. They will allow their day-to-day work tasks to dictate their agenda, which will in turn cause them and their organizations to underperform and not accomplish all that they could.

There is so much at stake here as we address the chronic shortage of strategic leaders. My hope for you and those you serve is that you will successfully escape the tactical tsunami and can offer greater strategic leadership to increase your influence and impact.

1.

CREATING VALUE

What Do You Provide That Others Value?

"Try not to become a man of success, but rather try to become a man of value."

–Albert Einstein

Noah Weber (not his real name) of Germany stood on the beach in Thailand as the tsunami approached, unable to do anything to save his life. He simply had not had enough warning. In Sendai, Japan, by contrast, Professor Kensuke Watanabe had the tools he needed to see the bigger picture. He had been notified of the earthquake and the impending tsunami, allowing him and his students time to get under their desks to avoid the falling earthquake debris and then to make it to higher ground before the tsunami water struck. From this elevation, they could see the bigger picture of the disaster that was unfolding below them.

In his book, *Ghosts of the Tsunami* (2017), Richard Lloyd Parry tells the story of Okawa Elementary School. Like the students, teachers, and administrators in nearby Sendai, Japan, those at this school could have escaped to higher ground. Unfortunately, because of poor leadership, they did not, and nearly everyone perished. In certain situations, strategic leadership can mean the difference between life and death. For your organization and mine, it can make the difference between success and failure.

Strategic leadership is present when people see the big picture of what matters most for those whom they serve. This leadership is needed everywhere around us, from senior leaders as well as from those who lead at lower levels. Let's begin the quest for strategic leadership with the most important concept for every organization: creating value for others.

WHY IT MATTERS

Creating value is not only at the core of every business and organizational endeavor: it is also significant in every relationship. Yes, this is a bold statement, but it has repeatedly been found to be a powerful concept. Value creation happens when we provide benefits that are important to others. In our professional lives, when we don't offer things that people appreciate, they stop buying our products and services. In our personal life, when we don't add something to the relationship, people may decide that they don't need another high-maintenance friend.

HOW IT WORKS

Creating value benefits your stakeholders and those around you through personal relationships, professional teamwork, and organizational transactions (both financial and non-financial). We will explore several elements of this concept here.

Creating Value is Our Core Engine

Our most important work personally, professionally, and organizationally (PPO) is to create value for others. We go to work for this purpose. The first chapter of Josh Kaufman's (2012) popular book, *The Personal MBA*, is entitled "Value Creation." He writes:

> Every successful business creates something of value. The world is full of opportunities to make other people's lives better in

some way, and your job as a businessperson is to identify things that people don't have enough of, then find a way to provide it.

The value you create can take on one of several different forms, but the purpose is always the same: to make someone else's life a little bit better.

Without value creation, a business can't exist—you can't transact with others unless you have something valuable to trade.

The best companies in the world are the ones that create the most value for other people.

Some businesses thrive by providing a little value to many, and others focus on providing a lot of value to only a few people. Regardless, the more real value you create for other people, the better your business will be and the more prosperous you'll become. (para. 37)

Without value creation, a business can't exist.

When I ask students about the purpose of business, their first answer is always, "to make money." They are wrong just like the people in the 1980s who said that the purpose of business was to increase shareholder value (stock price). The purpose of every for-profit and nonprofit organization today is to create value for their stakeholders. This is also true for you in your family relationships at home.

In her book, *What Management Is*, Joan Magretta of the Harvard Business School elaborates on the core function of creating value.

The fundamental job of management— creating value for customers by helping people to be more productive and innovative in a common effort— that hasn't changed one bit. **Value creation is the animating principle of modern management and its chief responsibility.** (2013, p.11)

Our goal is for you to see how creating value applies equally to for-profits, nonprofits, and your personal life. The goal of organizations today is to create value for their stakeholders. This enduring concept remains powerful in its broad applications.

The purpose of every organization today is to create value for their stakeholders.

The power of this creating value concept is its ability to explain so much of what happens in life and leadership. Here are some examples:

- **Customers and those we serve:** A company and organization is only successful to the extent that it provides something that others value.
- **Employment:** In general, when you create more value than cost, you are employed and retained to create that value. Your value creation may come in the form of sales, services, scientific discoveries, manual labor, etc. Employees who can create more value than their peers are more likely to be retained and be promoted.
- **Raise:** When you create a lot more value than your employer expected, you may get a raise in your compensation in recognition of that value creation and as a retention incentive to continue that good work.
- **Firing:** When employees bring more cost than value to their organization, they are more likely to be fired. Their high cost could be salary. It could also be true that a person is "high maintenance," which is more relational than financial.
- **Relationships:** When people create value in relationships, they are more likely to find someone who wants to be

friends with them. How do you create value in a relationship? A highly-valued relationship is one that is supportive, interesting, stable, life-giving, fun, etc.

- **Serving Overseas:** Besides the US, I have lived and worked in three other countries for two or more years. I found that local people were glad I was there when I added value to their lives.

So, what do we learn from these examples?

- Creating value can be **financial**, both personal and organizational.
- Creating value can be **non-financial**, such as relationships, brand strength, morale, retention, etc.
- Creating value is central to both **for-profits and non-profits.**
- Value creation can relate to paid **employees** as well as volunteers. Even though they work for free, some **volunteers** can be very "costly."

Value is in the Eye of the Beholder

When the tsunamis in Japan and Southeast Asia struck, most people were looking down at their desks where they were working or down the street where they were walking. The only way to escape a tsunami is to look well outside of oneself. Those who had time and perspective were able to make an escape plan.

In the same way, if we want to know what we provide for others, we must look at our work from an outsider's point of view. In other words, our stakeholders decide if they value what we offer or not.

For example, my wife, Cheri, does not enjoy receiving cut flowers like roses. She would rather I spend that money on a rose bush that will last longer or on shared activities like travel. I can tell her to appreciate flower bouquets, but at the end of the day, it is her call, not mine.

Our stakeholders decide if they value
what we provide or not.

Outside-In or Inside-Out

We can take two approaches to creating value. An outside-in approach begins with the people out there, sometimes referred to as "the market," and seeks to understand what they need or want. Once we know what people value, we can:

- Provide what they want.
- Solve their problem.
- Address their pain points.

Southwest Airlines got its start in Texas by recognizing the need that people had to fly within Texas rather than to drive across such a large state. Once we clarify a need out there or a problem to be solved, we can go about addressing that need. An outside-in approach focuses primarily on people out there and not ourselves.

An inside-out approach begins by determining our core competencies. What products or services are we uniquely competent at or qualified to provide? Once we have clarity as to what we can offer, we can look for markets that need what we provide. Therefore, the inside-out approach begins with us and looks out to see where there is a need or desire for what we provide.

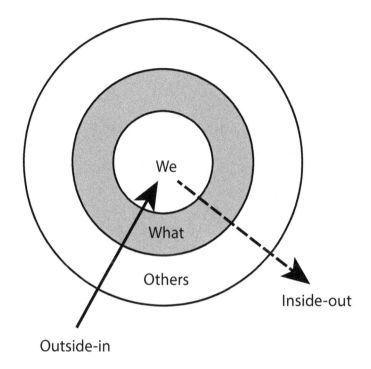

Outside-in

This above diagram shows both approaches. Outside-in looks at others and what we can provide that they value. Inside-out looks at what we can provide for others. Every person, team, and organization will want to consider outside-in and inside-out strategies for themselves personally and professionally as well as for their organizations.

Value Proposition(s)

The classic value proposition lies at the heart of value creation. It addresses the question, "What do you provide for whom and at what cost/price?"

There are three key components here:

- **What** benefits and value are you providing?
- **Whom** – What stakeholders do you serve?
- **Cost/Price** - What are people paying?

Value Proposition: What do we provide for whom and at what cost/price?

Comparison and Contrast of Two Value Propositions

Value propositions are put forth in the marketplace every day. It is important to remember that these concepts relate to customers and employees, employers and employees, as well as to for-profits and nonprofits.

Let's compare two sets of value propositions. For example, I am a frequent flyer and usually fly Delta or Southwest. They have two different value propositions. Delta is a full-service global airline while Southwest is more of a short-haul domestic airline with lower fares. Though these two airlines provide different value propositions, they are nonetheless two of the largest and most successful airlines in the United States.

Both airlines have both customers and employees that they need to satisfy in order to be successful.

Delta

Delta's value proposition is to provide comprehensive global services for its customers, especially high-end customers. Delta offers first-class services to business travelers to every part of the world. They have travel lounges in global airports. When I travel to Asia, it is on Delta.

Besides customers, Delta also has pilots. What is Delta's value proposition to its pilots? It offers traditional pay, opportunities, and the possibility of long-haul flights.

Southwest

When Southwest Airlines started, it only flew in Texas and was an affordable alternative to driving. Today, Southwest is known as loveable, affordable, and flexible. When I first moved to Nashville, I flew Delta in the US. Eventually, I saw the benefits of Southwest. It had more nonstop flights for me instead of Delta's hub-spokes approach that always routed me through Atlanta. I also liked how I could easily change my flights on Southwest at the last minute without a fee. All these add up to Southwest's unique value proposition.

What is Southwest's value proposition to its pilots? In the early days, it was easier to get on with Southwest. Today, they are similar to other airlines like Delta in pay and benefits. However, they lack the opportunity to fly jumbo jets around the world. These long-haul opportunities pay better and provide opportunities to travel the world. On the other hand, Southwest does like to tout that unlike other airlines, they have never laid off pilots in 40 years.

As you can see, these two airlines have different value propositions both in the marketplace and to their pilots. While they are different, they have both been successful.

Let's take a look at how these value proposition concepts can also apply to nonprofits.

- **Organization to End-Users** – The Red Cross supplies people in need with free, safe blood.
- **Donor to Organization** – People donate safe and usable blood to the Red Cross for free. Success occurs when enough people feel this is a worthwhile cause to give both blood and financial donations. It fails when enough people do not feel compelled by the Red Cross's mission.
- **Organization to Donor** – The Red Cross provides people with a safe way to give without compensation. The Red Cross makes a clear and compelling case for why people should do this. They have a problem when the organization is not able to make this case to enough people.

Bringing More Value Than Cost

Once you understand the foundational concepts of value creation and value propositions, they can become the core of how you think, live and lead. You can also extend these concepts to employment and your career. When employees bring more value than cost, their companies want to keep them. When employees bring more cost than value, there is a problem. At all PPO levels (personal, professional, and organizational), things go well when people and organizations bring more value than cost. Things don't go well when it is apparent that people bring more cost than value. These concepts can apply to financial costs, such as salaries, as well as to non-financial costs, such as relationships.

When an employee brings more cost than value,
there is a problem.

WHAT TO DO NEXT

The first pillar of strategic leadership is to understand how value is created. These principles can be applied to almost every role and at all PPO levels (personal, professional, and organizational).

- **Personal**: We create value for others through personal relationships as we listen well, provide support and encouragement, contribute insight, and financial support.
- **Professional**: We create value for those with whom we work by getting work done, leading teams well, providing creativity, and managing resources.
- **Organizational**: Companies and organizations create value in the marketplace through the products and services they offer.

Personal

Do you have friends? When you create value for others, they will be more favorable toward their relationship with you. On the other hand, you may have had "high maintenance" friends—people who bring more cost than value.

While we have commitments to family members that may transcend this concept, the relationship between value and cost tends to still apply. If you have a relative who brings a lot of value to your relationship, you will want to spend more time with them. If you have other relatives that are consistently problematic, you will typically want to spend less time with them. For example, I have a family member who has opinions on everything and talks incessantly. I have to admit that I try to avoid them.

Professional

Creating value applies to both our personal and professional lives. Do you earn a wage at a company or organization? If so, it is because you provide value that they feel is worth paying for.

Take a few minutes and write out your value creation and value propositions. Answer these questions:

- **What do you provide?** What benefits do you offer to your customers and employer?
- **That others value?** Who are your different stakeholders and what do you provide to each one?
- **At what cost/price?** What price do your customers pay for what you do? What is the cost (financial and non-financial) to your employer for what you do?

The clearer you can be on these items, the better you can serve those around you. If you are not sure about all of the details, just try to write down the main ideas.

Keep in mind that the better your value creation and value proposition(s), the happier your customers and employer will be. With almost any endeavor, the stronger your value proposition, the more customers you will have in the marketplace. When you offer a stronger value proposition to employers, you are more likely to have more, higher-paying job opportunities.

Organizational

While value creation applies to us as individuals, it also applies to our organizations. My university, Trevecca, offers an MBA program. Recently, I discussed creating value with a group of new students. Students consistently tell us that we create unique value for them compared to other programs because our MBA program is:

- **Easy to Access** – We don't require the GMAT for admissions.
- **Affordable** – Total costs for the 2018 program are less than $25,000 as opposed to Vanderbilt, which lists at $125,000.
- **Designed for Working Adults** – Classes are available one night a week or 100% online.
- **Christian in its Foundations** – We seek to integrate biblical faith into all of our courses and interactions.

We have been able to create value for students such that as of 2018, we enroll about 300 new students each year, resulting in Trevecca's status as one of the largest MBA programs in the state of Tennessee.

What product or services does your organization have in the marketplace? Are these offerings growing or declining? Remember what we said earlier, value is in the eye of the beholder. Customers decide what it is that they value.

Take some time to write down the value propositions your organization has in the marketplace. They don't have to be perfect—start with something that you can later refine yourself and with others.

We began this chapter with the question, "What do you provide that others value?" In the next two chapters, we will address the "you" and the "others" of this question.

30 MINUTES THIS WEEK

Jot down what you provide for others that they value. The process of writing this down will grow your strategic leadership. If you have more time down the road, you can re-work the wording, and you can talk it through with some others on your team.

Dedicate 10-30 minutes each week to reviewing what you provide that others value at all three PPO levels and how you might increase that created value.

- Personal
- Professional
- Organizational

2.

DEVELOPING SELF-AWARENESS

How Are You Unique?

"You can't get away from yourself by moving from one place to another."

–Ernest Hemingway

As mentioned earlier, each of the two epic tsunamis in Southeast Asia and Japan had unique characteristics. In *Ghosts of the Tsunami*, Richard Lloyd Parry (2017) writes about how the local responses to the earthquake and ensuing tsunami in Japan were very much in keeping with the culture and identity of the Japanese people. The warning system and initial response were precise, fast, and orderly. At the same time, a crisis of this magnitude was well outside of the routine protocol for dealing with earthquakes. In several ways, their traditional responses were unfortunately inadequate.

Lloyd Parry provides an example of how traditional patterns of interaction in Japan overshadowed what needed to be done. He writes, "the experience of the generations, the reassurance of the ancestors— these beat louder in the blood than the voices from the loudspeaker cars, screeching, "Evacuate! Evacuate!" (2017, p. 139). The people here responded in ways that they knew, rather than heeding official warnings. For all of us, it is invaluable to know our default patterns of interaction so that we can know the strengths and weaknesses we bring to our lives, work, and leadership.

High self-awareness helps all leaders to live, lead, and serve better. On the importance of self-awareness, we read the following from Bill George (2007), the former CEO of Medtronic and now a popular professor at Harvard Business School:

> When the seventy-five members of the Stanford Graduate School of Business Advisory Council were asked to recommend the most important capability for leaders to develop, their answer was nearly unanimous: **Self-Awareness.** (George, 2007, p. 69)

WHY IT MATTERS

On the topic of self-awareness, Tasha Eurich (2018a) writes in HBR about the many favorable outcomes that result for those who possess high self-awareness.

> Self-awareness seems to have become the latest management buzzword—and for good reason. Research suggests that **when we see ourselves clearly, we are more confident and more creative.** We make sounder decisions, build stronger relationships, and communicate more effectively. We're less likely to lie, cheat, and steal. We are better workers who get more promotions. And we're more-effective leaders with more-satisfied employees and more-profitable companies. (para. 1)

When self-awareness is high, many good things follow. When self-awareness is low, it can have disastrous consequences. In "Working with People Who Aren't Self-Aware," Eurich writes:

Un-self-aware colleagues aren't just frustrating; they can cut a team's chances of success in half. According to our research, other consequences of working with unaware colleagues include increased stress, decreased motivation, and a greater likelihood of leaving one's job. (2018b, para. 3)

Research tells us that self-awareness clearly plays a critical role in both success and a lack of success.

HOW IT WORKS

Each person and organization has singular characteristics and creates value for their stakeholders in different ways. You should be able to articulate how you (individually and collectively) are unique and how you and your organization uniquely create value for others.

Earlier, we asked the question of "What do you provide that others value?" Self-awareness addresses the "you" in this statement. At the heart of self-awareness is the ability to perceive yourself on three different levels. As you understand yourself better, you can better manage your life, work, and leadership. These three different levels include:

- How you see yourself.
- How others see and experience you.
- How versatile you are at adapting to the need of the situation.

As you grow in self-understanding, you can add an understanding of how others see you as well as appreciate your versatility in being able to work outside your natural tendencies. Let's go into more detail on these three areas.

Understanding Yourself

Self-awareness is knowledge about yourself and includes a keen understanding of:

- Who you are.
- How you work.
- How your characteristics vary in different roles, situations,
  and stress levels.
- The unique value you create for others in personal relationships, professional relationships, and through leadership roles.

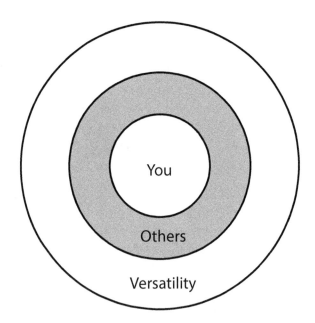

How You Can Grow in Self-Awareness

Self-awareness can be learned and developed. Here are some sugges-
tions for ways you can grow in your self-awareness:

- **Self-Reflection**: What do you like? What do you do well and what do you struggle with?
- **Structured Assessments**: DISC, Myers-Briggs (MBTI), StrengthFinders, etc.
- **Feedback from Others**: Family members, friends, co-workers, etc.

How Others Experience You

There may be some differences between how you see yourself and how others experience you. For example, while you may see yourself as introverted, you may also see yourself as thoughtful and collaborative. It is good to know whether others experience you as cool and aloof. We all want others to have a good experience with us in ways that align with our authentic self.

Versatility

It is not enough to know ourselves. We must also explore our versatility. For example, my Myers-Briggs personality type is ENTP, which means that I live and lead with certain tendencies. Versatility means that I am able to adjust and adapt when needed. While I am naturally analytical, I am not naturally organized. To maximize my value and contribution to others, I have had to get better at some things I am not naturally good at.

WHAT TO DO NEXT

Growing in self-awareness is a lifelong journey that never ends. As I now have new grandchildren, I am learning that good grandparenting is different from good parenting. While self-awareness is often discussed in terms of the individual, it applies to all three PPO levels (personal, professional, and organizational).

Personal

Begin by reflecting on who you are and how this plays out in your life, work, and leadership.

Use one or more popular assessments such as:
- ◦ Myers-Briggs (MBTI)
- ◦ DISC
- ◦ StrengthsFinder
- ◦ Enneagram

NOTE: There are inexpensive or free versions of some of the above. However, you may want review your results with a trained coach or someone certified in the assessment.

Talk with those around you and see what they say about your tendencies:
- ◦ Parents
- ◦ Spouse
- ◦ Children
- ◦ Co-workers
- ◦ Friends

As you grow in understanding of yourself personally, you can then look more closely at yourself in professional settings.

Professional

People I coach often ask what they should work on. While that varies by person, I often say that a good place to start is finding what you are good at and working on moving that to great.

Here I like to use the Good-to-Great Rubric (G2GR) which includes:

- Great
- Good
- Adequate
- Poor
- Train Wreck or Nonexistent

NOTE: We have a later chapter dedicated to the Good-to-Great Rubric.

You can take this Good-to-Great Rubric (G2GR) and apply it in the following ways.

- **Find what you are good at** and see if you can move from good to great. This will probably be your leading value contribution.
- **Find what you are poor at** and see if you can get to adequate. This will help you ensure that your weaknesses don't become significant distractions to your areas of contribution.

Remember, when you interview for a job, it is important to be able to articulate where you are good-to-great and where you are adequate and how these align with the value you can create in the workplace and in certain roles.

Organizational

Organizations, like people, cannot be good at everything, nor can they compete in every market. Each organization should ask itself how it is unique. This extends to each organization's unique value proposition.

Michael Porter, the greatest strategy expert of our generation, has created five tests of strategy:

- A unique value proposition
- A tailored value chain
- Trade-offs different from rivals
- Fit across the value chain
- Continuity over time

As you can see, the first test of good strategy is a unique value proposition. In your role as a growing strategic leader, you can help your team, department, and/or organization to clarify their unique value propositions. This is central to strategy and key to an organization's self-awareness.

30 MINUTES PER WEEK

Write down how you are unique in the value that you create for your stakeholders. For now, just jot down any thoughts that come to mind. I have my MBA students do this for themselves personally, professionally, and for their organization.

Once you have this written down, take some time each week to refine the language. Compare your notes and thoughts with others to see if they agree with you.

3.

ANALYZING STAKEHOLDER RELATIONSHIPS

Whom Do You Serve?

"If an organization has time to do only one thing when it comes to strategic planning that one thing ought to be a stakeholder analysis."

–John Bryson

"How did you think the meeting went?" the Managing Director asked.

"I think that everyone in the meeting was happy," I offered.

"So, you thought it went well?" he asked.

"No, I think it went poorly."

"Why would you say that?" he asked.

"They are happy with themselves. But they forget that they are not the primary stakeholders. They feel good about themselves, but the company continues to miss its sales goals and is in danger of closing. We need to spend some time with them reminding them that customers are their primary stakeholders."

Citizens of nearly fifty different countries lost their lives in the Christmas Tsunami disaster–Sweden and Germany alone each lost over 500 individuals. When it comes to deadly tsunamis, there are many stakeholders, including citizens, scientists, IT experts, governments, and more. Similarly, most of us have more stakeholders than we think.

Stakeholder analysis involves laying out your stakeholders and identifying your value proposition to each.

Who are the stakeholders in your world? Stakeholder analysis involves laying out your stakeholders and identifying your value proposition for each. When I was a college president, I used to say that I could easily neglect several stakeholder groups each day, such as students, faculty, staff, board members, vendors, and parents. Students wanted more of my time. Faculty wanted more of my time. Everybody wanted more of my time. It was important for me to discover what my value proposition was for each of these stakeholder groups. How could I create value for these groups given my resource limitations? I learned that my primary stakeholder group, students, enjoyed informal interaction across the campus. They didn't need a lot of time, but casual visibility and engagement were important. Faculty members were quite different. They were not looking for informal time together. They wanted me to address them at faculty meetings with a concise update on the most important issues that impacted their work. Knowing who your stakeholders are and what their expectations are of you is one of the keys to strategic leadership.

Stakeholder analysis gives us the tools we need for the important work of mapping commitments and expectations. Strategy expert John Bryson (2011) emphasizes the importance of understanding stakeholders:

I usually argue that if an organization has time to do only one thing when it comes to strategic planning, that one thing ought to be a stakeholder analysis. **Stakeholder analyses are so critical because the key to success** in the public and nonprofit sectors—and the private sector, too, for that matter—**is the satisfaction of key stakeholders.** (p. 132)

WHY IT MATTERS

When we are not aware of stakeholders and their expectations, we have serious blind spots. For example, when a husband thinks everything in his marriage is fine, but his wife tells him she wants a divorce. Or when your boss tells you that you are being fired because you are inattentive to what he cares about most. When you fail to understand your stakeholder relationships, many negative consequences can result.

HOW IT WORKS

Stakeholders are those who have a "stake" in what you do personally, professionally, and organizationally. Stakeholder analysis happens when you identify your key stakeholders and your stated and unstated value propositions to each of them as well as any gaps in value delivery. Stakeholder analysis is not overly complex. It hinges on the **value proposition.** A value proposition answers the question, "What do you provide for whom and at what cost/price?" Stakeholder analysis focuses on the "whom" of this value proposition.

---

*Value Proposition: What do you provide for **whom** and at what cost/price?*

Imagine the following exchange between a hotel guest and a front desk attendant:

"I was expecting more. At a Hilton resort, we are paying top dollar and this service is only so-so."

"I am sorry, sir. We will immediately address this service problem. We are committed to meeting and exceeding your expectations."

Clarity on value propositions helps to identify any gaps between what you promise to deliver and what the client or customer receives.

Value propositions can be applied to both financial and non-financial relationships. For example, as the MBA director at my university, I have teamed up with others to create financial value for the university by increasing enrollment from two cohort starts per year to over fifteen per year. I also create non-financial value for the Dean of the Business School through our personal and professional relationship. During my annual evaluation this year, I asked him how I could increase the value I create for him and the business school. One way that I did so in 2018 was through my work in developing and directing our new Doctor of Business Administration (DBA) Program. Non-financially, I seek to be a low-maintenance friend and colleague with the other faculty in the business school. Beyond my faculty position, I have other personal and professional stakeholders I can map out.

In the same way, you can begin your formal stakeholder analysis by asking "Whom do we serve?" Identify those who have a "stake" in your endeavor. Here are some examples of stakeholders:

- Customers, clients, patients, students, etc.
- End users / those we serve (nonprofits)
- Employees
- Vendors
- Owners
- Boards and Board Members
- Donors (nonprofits)
- Communities

The many stakeholders we have can be separated into three different categories:

- Primary
- Secondary
- Foundational

Primary Stakeholders

We begin by asking "For whom does our company or organization primarily exist?"

One day, my wife, Cheri, said to me, "Now I understand the similarities between colleges and hospitals." Cheri is a veteran healthcare provider with over 20 years of experience.

"What is that supposed to mean?" I asked.

"The doctors are the only ones that matter," she stated.

"I'm still confused. What does that mean?" I replied.

"Often, at hospitals, the doctors are considered more important than the patients," she explained. "At colleges, sometimes the faculty are viewed as more important than the students. See, hospitals and colleges are similar, the doctors are the only ones that matter."

Cheri was seeing something here that is very important. Colleges must realize that students are their primary stakeholders, not faculty. In a recent episode of *60 Minutes*, the host interviewed the president of one of the largest universities in the United States to discuss innovation in higher education. The university president stated that a large shift is currently underway as institutions are moving from viewing faculty as their primary stakeholder to viewing students as their primary stakeholder. Who is your primary stakeholder? For hospitals, this would be patients. For Best Buy, that would be customers. For schools, this is students.

More often than you might think, people make the mistake of believing that employees or even the owners of private companies are an organization's primary stakeholders. In most cases, it is best to think of primary stakeholders as the organization's customer or end-user and to see employees as secondary stakeholders.

Secondary Stakeholders

Secondary stakeholders are important, but they are also frequently overlooked. Secondary stakeholders offer support services to primary stakeholders. Secondary stakeholders can include:

- Supervisor
- Employees
- Vendors
- Board members (nonprofits)
- Communities
- Donors (nonprofits)

When employees or other secondary stakeholders are treated poorly, service to primary stakeholders often declines as well.

"How long will the wait be?" I asked the hostess as I walked into the restaurant.

"About 30 minutes" she replied.

I turned to my wife. "Cheri, why is there a 30-minute wait when that whole section is empty?" I whispered.

"It is because they are under-staffed," she explained. "Some of their employees must not have shown up tonight."

When your employees are not doing well, your primary stakeholders, such as customers, may suffer. While they are not primary stakeholders, every secondary stakeholder in your supply chain can impact your overall effectiveness.

Foundational Stakeholders

While classical stakeholder analysis focuses on primary and secondary stakeholders, foundational stakeholders including families, friends, and faith, must be taken into account.

"Rick, I need to share something personal with you," said one of our VPs.

"What's that?"

"Bill and I are getting divorced," she continued.

"I am sorry to hear that."

"I was totally shocked. He came home one day and said that all I cared about was work and he was tired of it."

At that moment, I realized that Megan had served our team well with dedication and sacrifice, but that she had neglected other important stakeholders in her life.

To those who have a strong faith background, God is a foundational stakeholder. Mother Teresa used to insist that the people she served were not her first concern. She once said, "No, I wouldn't touch a leper for a thousand pounds; yet I willingly cure him for the love of God." God was her first and foundational stakeholder.

WHAT TO DO NEXT

A good place to start with stakeholder analysis is to list your primary, secondary, and foundational stakeholders. This will often include four to eight stakeholder groups. For each group, list your value proposition for that group. Then try and describe where the gaps are in fulfilling that value proposition.

For example, an airline like Southwest might have a value proposition of "providing safe, on-time travel at an affordable price." We could then ask about Southwest's safety record, on-time arrival percentage, and its prices compared to its competitors. This analysis would be helpful in identifying any value delivery gaps. Value delivery gaps are the differences between the promise of our value proposition and the actual experience of the stakeholder. Let's work through your stakeholders in your personal, professional, and organizational settings.

Personal

Begin by listing your foundational stakeholders. Who is important in your world when it comes to family, friends, and faith?

Next, you can ask yourself how you create value for these stakeholders. Don't worry if this is difficult to do at first, as we don't often think of personal relationships in this way. Personally, I highly value my relationship with my wife, Cheri. She values exercise, prayer, time together, and the outdoors. To bring greater value to our relationship, I often accompany her on a walk or run outside. This also provides an opportunity for us to spend time together and pray together. Once we have reviewed the stakeholders in our personal lives, we can move to our professional lives.

Professional

"Steve, I am sorry to say that we are going to have to let you go," said his supervisor.

"Wow, I didn't see this coming. I am meeting my numbers. What's the issue?" Steve responded.

"We have daily check-ins and you are often late. We place a high value on punctuality here and you are not meeting our standards," his boss explained.

While Steve understood that his primary stakeholders were his sales customers, he seemed to neglect a very important secondary stakeholder: his boss. Steve wasn't paying attention and it ultimately cost him his job.

List your professional stakeholders and the accompanying value propositions for each person/group. For example, what do you provide to your boss that they value? At my annual evaluation last month, I asked my boss this very question. Stakeholders in our personal and professional lives relate to us as individuals. Organizations also have their sets of stakeholders.

Organizational

Begin by asking what your company or organization brings to particular markets. These primary stakeholders are your customers, clients, students, etc. Consider the following statements by employees.

"We have such a great team!"

"We were just voted one of the top places to work in our region."

"I can't understand why our revenues continue to drop."

The above shows the involvement of several stakeholders. While employees seem to be doing well, they were missing something significant with their customers either through products, customer service, or some other factor.

30 MINUTES PER WEEK

Begin by listing your stakeholders in all three PPO areas (personal, professional, and organizational). Then, write down your value proposition(s) for each stakeholder, answering the question, "What do you provide and at what price/cost?" If you struggle with that level of detail, just start with "what do you provide that they value?" Next, quickly write down how it is going using the Good-to-Great Rubric of Great-Good-Adequate-Poor-Nonexistent. We discuss the Good-to-Great Rubric in more detail in a later chapter.

4.

ELEVATING YOUR STRATEGIC ALTITUDE

At What Altitude Do You Lead?

"Hope is not a strategy."

–Vince Lombardi

Earlier, we discussed how strategic leadership affected Okawa Elementary School during the 2011 tsunami in Japan. Let's look at how leadership impacted the school in more detail.

As the earthquake hit, the children were directed to gather on the school playground, in accordance with the school's policy for dealing with a crisis. About 30 minutes later, when two boys suggested heading to a nearby hill for safety, they were told to get back in line, which they did. They ultimately perished. Shortly thereafter, as the children lined up to walk across the street, two other boys made a break for the nearby hill. They survived. In this case, seeing and acting like everyone else had tragic consequences. Those who saw the need to move above the approaching tsunami survived. Strategic leadership is about seeing the need to work and lead at a higher level, thus escaping the tactical tsunami of everyday work.

Strategic leaders who work at a higher level are relatively rare. In a *Forbes* (2010) article entitled "The Three Strengths of a True Strategic Leader," Kate Beatty writes:

Statistics show that **fewer than 10% of leaders exhibit strategic skills,** a woefully inadequate number considering the demands on organizations today...The job of strategy is not limited to a few top executives. Strategic leaders are needed throughout our organizations if they are to adapt, innovate and succeed well into the future. (para. 1)

In their book, *Becoming a Strategic Leader* (2013), Beatty and her Center for Creative Leadership colleagues Richard Hughes and David Dinwoodie write:

Strategic leaders propel their organizations through successive iterations of a learning process with strategic thinking, strategic acting, and strategic influencing skills. These skills are needed in every element of the learning process, and leaders at every level in the organization can practice them. (p. 4)

Taking your leadership to the next level includes a strong understanding of the different levels of engagement.

WHY IT MATTERS

When organizations are filled with typical tactical workers and leaders, work gets done. The problem is that people are often over-worked, while strategic goals and outcomes are missed or neglected. Only when strategic leaders rise to the challenge are teams and organizations able to focus attention on their strategic goals and outcomes. The goal is not to work harder. The goal is to advance what is most important.

HOW IT WORKS

The key need of strategic altitude is understanding first that work and leadership function at different altitudes. Some high-level leaders are very visionary in that they are both inspirational and aspirational. We need this kind of leadership. Once we understand the range and features of strategic altitude from high-level visionary leadership to on-the-ground tactical leadership, we can seek to understand where you fit into that scale as well as the mix of leaders in your organization.

Different Altitudes of Engagement

When we refer to strategic altitude, we usually break it down into three different levels. Next to each level is a percentage that represents those in that level.

- Visionary Level (~15%)
- Strategic Level (<10%)
- Tactical Level (~75%)

You can see here that the majority of people work and lead at the tactical level. Tactical people like on-the-ground, practical work. The next largest group are visionary leaders, individuals who dream big. They are inspirational and aspirational. The smallest group are strategic leaders. They focus on how to connect tactical work with visionary aspirations. Each of these altitudes has different features. To future help you understand these levels, we will explore each in more detail.

Visionary Level

The visionary level is the highest level of engagement and refers to the core concepts of who we are as an organization including:

- **Vision** – Where we are headed or a picture of our preferred, aspirational future.
- **Values** – Who are we and what do we want to be known for?
- **Value Propositions** – Here, we look at what we are providing to whom and at what cost/price.

This visionary level of engagement is the starting point for all that we do because our vision, values, and value propositions are at our very core. Once we clarify our work at the highest visionary level, we can move to mid-level strategy.

Strategic Level

If vision is about aspirational direction, strategy is about deciding how we are going to get there. President Kennedy dreamed of reaching the moon. NASA had to develop the strategies to achieve that vision. Strategic choices require prioritization. Which road will we take to reach our preferred destination, and what are our mid-range strategies to support those priorities? We also have to choose which metrics we will use as short-term and long-term measures of progress. Lastly, with limited resources, which initiatives will provide the most strategic return on investment? Great strategies give us greater confidence that our vision can be advanced.

Tactical Level

Tactical engagement is about our practical, everyday work. That said, it takes on new importance as we seek to align our tactical work with our visionary and strategic levels. Tactical work becomes about executing and implementing our strategy by doing the right work well. Strategic altitude is central to all that we do.

Finding the Right Mix

Most people have a preferred altitude with two secondary altitudes. Strategic leaders are active in helping organizations to advance what they care about most. At the same time, they need to have adequate or better vision as well as adequate or better tactical skills.

For example, Alex's team is responsible for growing the revenue of his organization. He is very good at understanding his organization's value proposition in the marketplace and the strategy needed to move this forward. At the visionary level, he needs to inspire the team to attain their aspirational goals. On a tactical level, he needs to organize his work and that of the team to maximize their effectiveness. Every leader needs to know their preferred level and be at least adequate at the other two levels.

WHAT TO DO NEXT

There are many places in which strategic altitude plays a vital role for both individuals and organizations.

Personal

As noted in an earlier chapter, self-awareness is critical. Therefore, the best place to start examining strategic altitude is with yourself. At what altitude do you feel most comfortable working and leading? Most people place themselves on the scale from very high visionary to on-the-ground tactical. Some people are visionary-strategic or strategic-tactical. Almost no one is a great visionary leader and a great tactical leader. I have known only a handful of leaders who are capable across the continuum. Personal insights on your strategic altitude can also be applied to your professional life.

Professional

How is your natural altitude affecting your professional work and leadership? Are you functioning well at the altitude that is most needed? If you are an admin, you probably don't need to bring visionary leadership as your primary contribution, although strategic leadership for admins can be very valuable.

In his book, *A Force for Change: How Leadership Differs from Management* (1990a), John Kotter writes that most organizations are over-managed and under-led. This gets to the heart of the reality that most managers are more tactical than strategic.

You can also look at your vocational future through this lens. If you are a strong visionary and strategic leader, you may want to look at higher level roles in your organization or another where your gifts could be used in more significant ways. While it is natural to see how strategic altitude applies to individuals, it can also be applied at the organizational level.

Organizational

The applications of strategic altitude for organizations are slightly different than for individuals. In strategic planning projects, we often begin by establishing strategic clarity at the visionary level. Once that has been clarified, we turn to strategies that will advance the organizational vision. Finally, we look at how tactical, on-the-ground work and projects can be aligned with upper-level vision and strategies.

30 MINUTES PER WEEK

Look at your typical week and assess how much time you spend focused on the visionary, strategic, and tactical levels. Make sure that you are spending at least 30 minutes a week at the strategic level, looking at the big issues that are affecting you and your organization the most.

If you want to drill down on this more, keep a time log for a few weeks and see how you use your time. This can be transformational for your professional life.

5.

LEVERAGING THE GOOD-TO-GREAT RUBRIC

Are You Getting Better?

*"However beautiful the strategy,
you should occasionally look at the results."*

–Winston Churchill

When both tsunamis hit in Southeast and East Asia, tens of thousands were instantly killed, while additional tens of thousands more were injured, some severely. In the midst of serious disasters, triage is an important tool. A publication of the World Health Organization (WHO) asserts that, "without a triage plan in place, resources are likely to be wasted—and more people are likely to die." Assessing how injured people are doing is the first step in deciding what level of care is needed.

About 15 years ago, when Jim Collins' book *Good to Great* (2005) was popular, an organization asked me if I could help them move from good to great. I replied that I would need some time to assess their situation. After a month, I had a clearer vision of the organization's needs. "Let's go from poor to adequate first," I proposed, "We can then worry about going from good to great later."

Thus was born the Good-to-Great Rubric (G2GR). It has been invaluable in many applications ever since. Let's see how you can put this rubric to work in your world.

WHY IT MATTERS

What are the two most important quotations in business? Dave Lavinsky (n.d.) says they come from longtime management guru Peter Drucker:

- "You can't manage what you don't measure." (para. 3)
- "Leadership is doing the right things." (para. 11)

Under-performing organizations struggle with both of these. On the other hand, higher-performing organizations have clarity on which measures matter and have a relentless commitment to results.

HOW IT WORKS

The G2GR provides us with a tool for more effectively assessing and communicating how things are going. It also deals with the courage needed to be honest with ourselves and others on how things are going.

Understanding the G2GR relates to the clear language and scales that can be used to assess the quality of a process, product, and service. For example, I was once asked by some organizational leaders what one problem I ran into the most with consulting. I answered by saying, "The inability or unwillingness to consistently differentiate between good-to-great work as compared to poor-to-adequate. People have a high tolerance for adequate and poor work." If you and your team use this rubric consistently, there is a good chance that your performance and that of your team will improve because you will have greater clarity on what results matter most in advancing your work. If you don't have clarity on measures that matter and track them consistently, you will often under-achieve. In brief, the G2GR has five points:

- Great
- Good
- Adequate
- Poor
- Train Wreck or Nonexistent

This simple graphic that can help us to see this visually.

5. Great (Exceeds Expectations)

4. Good (Meets Expectations)

3. Adequate (Below Expectations)

2. Poor (Well Below Expectations)

1. Train Wreck (Not Present)

Measures that Matter

Not every measure or metric is equally important. Strategic leaders are willing and able to pinpoint key metrics that drive important outcomes. In his popular book, *Measure What Matters* (2018), John Doerr discusses how measures came to prominence for Andy Grove, the CEO of Intel, as well as for Google founders Larry Page and Sergey Brin. Doerr writes:

> Long before Gmail or Android or Chrome, Google brimmed with big ideas. The founders were quintessential visionaries, with extreme entrepreneurial energy...They would need timely, relevant data. To track their progress. To measure what mattered. (pp. 5-6)

There is much that could be said about measuring what matters with all its accompanying detail, but I suggest that regularly using the G2GR is a good place to start. One of the reasons that this rubric is so helpful is because it is very intuitive. Most people know the differences between these descriptors and that good is different from great and poor is below adequate.

This rubric also fits closely with the common 1-5 Likert scale. Therefore, I often suggest that you use the following numbers:

5 = Great
4 = Good
3 = Adequate
2 = Poor
1 = Nonexistent

This numerical scheme works well when aggregating data. I can ask ten people about three different hotels and then aggregate and average the data. Hotel A is 4.3. Hotel B is 3.5, and Hotel C is 2.8. You can also say that last year, our communication was assessed at 3.5 but this year it is up to a 4.1.

Another variation that we often use in surveys is to change the labels to:

5 = Strongly Agree
4 = Agree
3 = Neutral
2 = Disagree
1 = Strongly Disagree

When you use this in a simple survey like those designed with Survey-Monkey, the program can automatically assign the number to agreement phrases. Here are a couple of example survey questions:

Our team manages their budget well.
5 = Strongly Agree
4 = Agree
3 = Neutral
2 = Disagree
1 = Strongly Disagree

The Vice President actively supports diversity.
5 = Strongly Agree
4 = Agree
3 = Neutral
2 = Disagree
1 = Strongly Disagree

Some groups like using different labels such as:
5 = Exceeds Expectations
4 = Meets Expectations
3 = Below Expectations
2 = Problems
1 = Significant Problems

Lastly, most groups in most situations tend to gravitate toward Good or 4. This works well. Most people know that Great is above Good and Adequate is below Good. Good tends to be that which is expected. The biggest problems people encounter using the G2GR are not the mechanics. Rather, they struggle with finding the courage to act on what they discover.

Courage

Though assessing performance can be relatively straightforward, leaders may be unwilling to address obvious issues. When I ask clients about under-performing workers and teams, they usually have quick, clear insight on their problem areas. When I ask what they are planning on doing about them, they often say, "not much."

It takes courage and time to address under-performing segments of your own work and those of your organization. I have encountered this with so many organizations that I wrote a blog post that explores this subject in more detail called "Performance Doesn't Matter." It can be found at www.clariontoolbox.com.

In *Measure What Matters*, you will see that much of the content is not about data and systems but rather about courage and culture. A good deal of the *Measure What Matters* book is about Andy Grove, former Intel CEO and 1997 TIME Man of the Year. Grove is famous for saying, "Complacency breeds failure. Only the paranoid survive" (Ibarra, 2016, para. 1).

Do we have the courage to address complacency and under-performance? The answer to this question may mean the difference between a future for our work and organization or not. Begin using this simple rubric in your life and organization. Over time, you will develop more insight and confidence.

WHAT TO DO NEXT

The uses for the G2GR are almost endless. It can easily be integrated into our personal, professional, and organizational lives and leadership.

Personal

First of all, you can use the G2GR to assess how things are going in your personal life. Here are a few example areas:

- Your exercise habits
- Your eating habits
- Your EQ skills
- And the list can go on and on

You can also use it as a common language with others. For example, you can talk with your roommate about a date you had on Friday night. "Wow, that was only adequate. Won't do that again." Obviously, adequate is different than poor or train wreck. You can also apply the G2GR to your work as you ask yourself, "What would a great, good, adequate, or poor job look like compared to my current job?" This reflection can help you to more easily assess things around you. As you gain confidence in using the G2GR, you can move forward by using it in your professional life.

Professional

As an individual professional and/or team leader, you can use this rubric to assess how things are going. For example, you can ask yourself, "How did I do on that project?" You can assess the effectiveness of those who report to you or those for whom you are responsible.

I often ask leaders that I coach, "Who are your great performers and who are your poor performers?" Not only does it help to mentally clarify how people are doing, I often ask them to do something about it. Many of the leaders and organizations I work with treat everyone the same. While it is important to treat everyone with equal respect, equal treatment can lead to the realization at the organizational level that performance doesn't matter. I encourage these team leaders to do more to recognize good-to-great work and more to address poor work. This is hard, but it can be transformational for morale and performance.

Lastly, you can adopt the G2GR as a common language in team settings. Pick 3-5 areas to discuss with your team. For example:

- How would you describe the usefulness of our weekly team meeting?
- How are we doing with our communication?
- How did we do last year in meeting our revenue goals?

When Alan Mulally came in as CEO to turn around Ford Motor Company, he started holding regular staff meetings. He would go around the table and each executive would say how things were going (Hoffman, 2013). Meeting after meeting, everyone said that things were good. One day, Mulally had had enough:

> "We're going to lose billions of dollars this year," he said, eyeing each executive in turn. "Is there anything that's not going well here?" Nobody answered. (p. 122)

Then, one day one of the managers admitted things were going poorly.

> There was dead silence. Everyone turned toward Fields. So did Mulally, who was sitting next to him. ...Suddenly, someone started clapping. It was Mulally. "Mark, that is great visibility," he beamed. "Who can help Mark with this?" (p. 124)

As a professional, it takes courage to speak up and say when things are not great or not even good. We will only get better if we are willing to be honest in describing what's not going well. As has often been said, there are no solutions if there are no problems. This doesn't apply exclusively to our professional lives–it can also make a big impact on the life of your organization.

Organizational

Strategic clarity is an excellent place for strategic leaders to begin using the G2GR. The areas are as follows:

- **Mission** – Do you have clarity on why you exist?
- **Vision** – Do you have a clear picture of your preferred future?
- **Values** – Are we in agreement on what we care about most?
- **Priorities** – Do we have clarity on our current 2-4 big deals?
- **Metrics** – Do you have a good set of metrics that tell you about your strategic progress?

If you discuss the above with your team or your organization and the feeling is that strategic clarity is adequate or poor, you have lots of company. Sometimes the clarity is good to great at the senior level, but our research tells us that as one moves from the top of an organization down through the ranks, strategic clarity usually decreases. From here, you can proceed by discussing a whole host of topics applying the G2GR as you go.

30 MINUTES PER WEEK

To what extent do you have language and concepts for differentiating quality? Do you have common language and processes that can help with this? Try out the G2GR and see if it can help clarify what quality looks like, and then use it to improve individual, team, and organizational performance.

CONCLUSION

Today, much of the northeast coast of Japan and the shores of Southeast Asia have been rebuilt. While debris has been cleared and many buildings have been rebuilt, the thinking of the affected people will never be the same.

WHY IT MATTERS

Reading this book will not instantly make you a strategic leader, but I hope that it will forever change your thinking about your life, work, and leadership.

As you go forward on the journey of strategic leadership, you now do so with a new set of tools that can help you to live, work, and lead with greater strategic leadership:

- Clarity on who you are and how you are unique.
- Clarity on the value you create for others.
- Clarity on the vision of the difference you can make.
- Greater courage in seeing the differences between good and great as well as poor and adequate.

Learning these concepts is not enough. Progress comes through putting them into practice.

HOW IT WORKS

Research tells us that strategic leadership can be developed. In the early pages of this book, we said that the development of strategic leaders can be accelerated by:

- Gaining strategic leadership **insight.**
- **Practicing** in real world settings.
- **Getting coached** by others.

These tools will not be of much help to you if you don't put them into practice.

WHAT TO DO NEXT

With 30 minutes per week or two hours per month as well as by integrating this thinking into your daily work, you can make significant progress.

My hope is that you will not continue your strategic leadership journey alone, but that you will take many people with you. As you seek to bless more people more, the larger world around you will be a better place because of your strategic leadership. If there is anything we at ClarionStrategy can do to help you on this journey, please let us know. Next, you may want to continue by reading *Building Strategic Organizations: The First Five Tools for Strategy and Strategic Planning.*

Blessings on your journey ahead.

Rick Mann, 2018

APPENDIX A

HOW TO USE THIS BOOK

This book was designed and written with clarion (pun intended) intentionality. First, this book was designed to be short and to the point. You can read this book in a weekend or even in an evening. Second, these are enduring topics. You could read this book every year for the rest of your life and gain new insights each time. Third, this book is designed for everyone. For experienced leaders, this will just reinforce and clarify what you may already know and practice. For tactical and practical workers, even those just out of college, this book can help you raise the altitude of your life, work, and leadership. Lastly, this book was designed to be practical. You can put these concepts into practice today, next week, or next year.

You can use this book with:

- **Yourself** – Professional Development
- Your **Team** – Team Development
- Your **Organization** – Organizational Development

Therefore, you can pass on this copy to someone who could benefit from it. You could also get a copy for all your direct reports or for all those in your company. This will give you some common language and concepts that you can use to build more strategic leaders and a strategic organization.

Personal, Professional, and Organizational (PPO)

As mentioned in the preface, and unlike many strategy and leadership books, this book was designed to be applied to your **personal** and **professional** life as well as to the larger issues of your company or **organization**. Therefore, remember to work through all five chapters at each of the three PPO levels (personal, professional, and organizational).

APPENDIX B

GETTING COACHING HELP

One way to escape the tactical tsunami is by moving to higher ground. You can make this journey on your own, but most people do better when coached by others.

Being coached by others can take on several forms including:

- Working for a **Coaching Leader**
- Partnering with a **Peer Coach**
- Hiring a **Professional Coach**

Each of these paths has pros and cons. Look over these and see which one may be right for you at this time.

WORKING FOR A COACHING LEADER

Some people are fortunate to work for a leader who is good at coaching others. This can be a great opportunity, but it also has some downsides.

Pros
It can be exciting and interesting to work for someone who is good at coaching. They can help you to learn as you go, providing you with good questions, empowerment, and support as you grow in your leadership.

Cons

This arrangement is known as a dual relationship, as your supervisor seeks to balance your development with the work that needs to be done. Maintaining this balance can be tricky at times. Also, just because you have a coaching leader in this job doesn't mean that you will have one in your next job.

Suggestions

If this relationship comes together naturally, that's great. That said, don't put too much pressure on yourself or on your supervisor to make it work.

PARTNERING WITH A PEER COACH

Another effective option can be to find a peer coach. Sometimes this is a friend or co-worker who can walk with you on your journey of growth and development without a fee. Some people do peer coaching in which one week you are coached by the person and the next week you coach them.

Pros

This can be affordable (free) and convenient if you have the right person to serve in this role.

Cons

Peer coaching can present a challenge when the person doesn't serve you well or you are ready to move on. The off-ramp can be awkward and can take a toll on your relationship.

Suggestions

There are lots of good people out there and you may be able to find someone who can do some peer coaching with you. You may want to start out by doing 3-4 sessions together and then re-evaluate after a month or two.

HIRING A PROFESSIONAL COACH

In this situation, as with finding a good counselor, you can interview possible coaches to find one that works for you at a rate that you can afford.

Pros

A qualified coach should be able to provide you with confidential, caring, and competent service. You can also make a change when the time seems right.

Cons

The main drawback of a professional coach is the cost, which can run anywhere from $100 to $800 per month for 2-4 sessions. Moreover, some coaches are only available via phone or Skype.

Suggestions

See what you want to accomplish, what you can afford, and who may be available. As graduate programs can run anywhere from $25,000 to $125,000, spending a few hundred or a few thousand dollars on coaching each year may bring the best Return on Investment (ROI) for you and your organization in your strategic leadership.

APPENDIX C

STRATEGIC ALTITUDE ASSESSMENT

Rank each of the following statements on a scale from 1-5 to see the features of your strategic altitude.

5 = Strongly Agree / 4 = Agree / 3 = Neutral / 2 = Disagree / 1 = Strongly Disagree

1. ___ You like working through a to-do list.
2. ___ You want to make sure things are done just right.
3. ___ You get tired of pie-in-the-sky dreamers.
4. ___ You don't like to be in a hurry.
5. ___ You find detailed work interesting.
6. ___ Those around you consider you inspirational.
7. ___ You have a strong and ever-present desire to change the world.
8. ___ You are much more interested and inspired by the big picture rather than the details.
9. ___ You get impatient in meetings that focus on details.
10. ___ You are aspirational and always want to take things to the next level.
11. ___ You have an extended track record of delivering high-level results.
12. ___ You regularly bring measurable clarity to important activities.

13. ___ You have consistently led important change in your team, departmental, or organizational settings.
14. ___ You take extra time and energy to try to understand the market forces working out there in regard to your work and that of your organization.
15. ___ You naturally think of the broader stakeholders who are affected by your work.

Once you have ranked all of these statements, total up your points in each of these following sections:

- Statements 1-5 – Tactical
- Statements 6-10 – Visionary
- Statements 11-15 – Strategic

You can then rank the order of your three levels and see what that says about the strategic altitude of your leadership.

APPENDIX D

RECOMMENDED READING

FOUNDATIONAL ARTICLES

Christensen, C. M. (2010). "How will you measure your life?"

Collis, D. J., & Rukstad, M. G. (2008). "Can you say what your strategy is?"

Kotter, J. P. (1995). "Leading change: Why transformation efforts fail."

Kotter, J. P. (1990). "What leaders really do."

Porter, M. E. (1990). "What is strategy?"

FOUNDATIONAL BOOKS

Collins, J. (2005). *Good to great and the social sectors.*

HBR's 10 must reads (boxed set). (2011).

HBR's 10 must reads on strategy. (2011).

Kotter, J. P. (2012). *Leading change.*

Lencioni, P. (2012). *The advantage: Why organizational health trumps everything else in business.*

McChesney, C., & Covey, S. (2012). *The 4 disciplines of execution: Achieving your wildly important goals.*

UPPER-LEVEL BOOKS

Hughes, R. L., Beatty, K. C., & Dinwoodie, D. L. (2014). *Becoming a strategic leader: Your role in your organization's enduring success* (2nd ed.).

Magretta, J. (2012). *Understanding Michael Porter: The essential guide to competition and strategy.*

Magretta, J., & Stone, N. (2013). *What management is: How it works and why it's everyone's business.*

Sloan, J. (2016). *Learning to think strategically* (3rd ed.).

NOTE: These resources can all be found in the References section of this book.

SUBSCRIBING TO HARVARD BUSINESS REVIEW

Over 30 years ago, I asked an internationally-known nonprofit leader what I should read. He said, "Read Harvard Business Review." I scoffed at his answer, saying to myself that I wanted to change the world and didn't have the time or the interest in reading HBR. In recent years, I went back to that leader and told him how dumb I was. Today, I read every HBR issue cover to cover. The topics covered are much broader than just business. Therefore, when people ask me what they should do if they don't have the time or the money for an MBA, I recommend HBR. For graduating MBA students who ask what they should do next, I say read HBR. That includes about everyone who wants to grow as a strategic leader.

For about $100 a year, you can get both the paper copy and digital access to current and past articles. HBR offers a treasure chest of insight on many business and non-business topics.

REFERENCES

Beatty, K. (2010, October 17). *The three strengths of a true strategic leader.* Retrieved from https://www.forbes.com/2010/10/27/three-strengths-strategy-leadership-managing-ccl.html#-3875ba115280

Bryson, J. M. (2011). *Strategic planning for public and nonprofit organizations* (4th ed.). San Francisco, CA: Jossey-Bass.

Christensen, C. M. (1997). *The innovator's dilemma: When new technologies cause great firms to fail.* Boston, MA: Harvard Business School Press.

Christensen, C. M. (2010). How will you measure your life? *Harvard Business Review, 88* (7/8), 46–51.

Christensen, C. M., Allworth, J., & Dillon, K. (2012). *How will you measure your life?* New York, NY: Harper Business.

Collins, J. (2005). *Good to great and the social sectors: Why business thinking is not the answer.* New York, NY: HarperCollins.

Collis, D. J., & Rukstad, M. G. (2008). Can you say what your strategy is? *Harvard Business Review, 86* (4), 82-90.

Doerr, J. (2018). *Measure what matters: How Google, Bono, and the Gates Foundation rock the world with OKRs.* New York, NY: Portfolio/Penguin.

Eurich, T. (2018, January 4). What self-awareness really is (and how to cultivate it). *Harvard Business Review.* Retrieved from https://hbr.org/2018/01/what-self-awareness-really-is-and-how-to-cultivate-it

Eurich, T. (2018, October 19). Working with people who aren't self-aware. *Harvard Business Review.* Retrieved from https://hbr.org/2018/10/working-with-people-who-arent-self-aware

George, B. & Sims, P. (2007). *True north: Discover your authentic leadership*. San Francisco, CA: Jossey-Bass.

HBR's 10 must reads (boxed set). (2011). Boston, MA: Harvard Business Review Press.

HBR's 10 must reads on leadership. (2011). Boston, MA: Harvard Business Review Press.

HBR's 10 must reads on strategy. (2011). Boston, MA: Harvard Business Review Press.

Hoffman, B. (2013). *American icon: Alan Mulally and the fight to save Ford Motor Company*. Sydney, Australia: Currency.

Hughes, R. L., Beatty, K. C., & Dinwoodie, D. L. (2014). *Becoming a strategic leader: Your role in your organization's enduring success* (2nd ed.). San Francisco, CA: Jossey-Bass.

Ibarra, H. (2016, April 11). Intel's Andy Grove and the difference between good and bad fear. *Financial Times*. Retrieved from https://www.ft.com/content/4c84d2e8-fa5f-11e5-8f41-df5bda8beb40

Johansen, B. (2012). *Leaders make the future: Ten new leadership skills for an uncertain world* (2nd ed.). San Francisco, CA: Berrett-Koehler.

Kaufman, J. (2012). *The personal MBA: Master the art of business*. New York, NY: Portfolio/Penguin.

Kotter, J. P. (1990a). *Force for change: How leadership differs from management*. Cambridge, MA: Free Press.

Kotter, J. P. (1990b). What leaders really do. *Harvard Business Review*, 68 (3), 103–111.

Kotter, J. P. (1995). Leading change: Why transformation efforts fail. *Harvard Business Review*, 73 (2), 59-67.

Kotter, J. P. (2012). *Leading change*. Boston, MA: Harvard Business Review Press.

Lavinsky, D. (n.d.). *The two most important quotes in business*. Retrieved from https://www.growthink.com/content/two-most-important-quotes-business

Leinwand, P., Mainardi, C., & Kleiner, A. (2015, December 30). *Only 8% of leaders are good at both strategy and execution.* Retrieved from https://hbr.org/2015/12/only-8-of-leaders-are-good-at-both-strategy-and-execution

Lencioni, P. (2012). *The advantage: Why organizational health trumps everything else in business.* San Francisco, CA: Jossey-Bass.

Lencioni, P. (2004). *Death by meeting: A leadership fable...About solving the most painful problem in business.* San Francisco, CA: Jossey-Bass.

Lloyd Parry, R. (2017). *Ghosts of the tsunami: Death and life in Japan's disaster zone.* New York, NY: Farrar, Straus and Giroux.

Magretta, J. (2012). *Understanding Michael Porter: The essential guide to competition and strategy.* Boston, MA: Harvard Business School Publishing.

Magretta, J., & Stone, N. (2013). *What management is: How it works and why it's everyone's business.* London, England: Profile Books.

McChesney, C. & Covey, S. (2012). *The 4 disciplines of execution: Achieving your wildly important goals.* New York, NY: Free Press.

Porter, M. E. (1990). What is strategy? *Harvard Business Review,* 74 (6), 61-78.

Schwartz, T. and McCarthy, C. (2007). Manage your energy, not your time. *Harvard Business Review,* 85 (10), 63–73. Retrieved from https://hbr.org/2007/10/manage-your-energy-not-your-time

Sinek, S. (2009). *Start with why: How great leaders inspire everyone to take action.* New York, NY: Portfolio/Penguin.

Sinek, S. (2010). *How great leaders inspire action* [Video file]. Retrieved from https://www.ted.com/talks/simon_sinek_how_great_leaders_inspire_action

Sloan, J. (2016). *Learning to think strategically* (3rd ed.). Burlington, MA: Butterworth-Heinemann.

The Thinkers50 Ranking. (n.d.). Retrieved from https://thinkers50.com/t50-ranking/

ABOUT THE AUTHOR

Rick Mann serves as Managing Director of ClarionStrategy, a small consulting firm that develops strategic leaders and strategic organizations that are able to more consistently deliver results and advance their missions.

At Trevecca Nazarene University in Nashville, TN, Rick serves as Professor of Leadership and Strategy as well as the director of the MBA and DBA programs, which enroll several hundred new students each year.

Previously Rick has served in a number of leadership roles in both the United States and overseas, including professor, program director, as well as provost and college president at Crown College (MN).

Rick received his MBA from the University of Minnesota, his MDiv from Ambrose University College (Canada), and his MA and PhD from Ohio State University.

Rick and Cheri live in Nashville, TN. Cheri is a nurse practitioner and works at a clinic for the underserved. Their mission each day is to bless more people more. For fun, they like to work out, travel to that next country, and enjoy the journey together. They have three married sons and a growing gang of grandchildren.

CPSIA information can be obtained
at www.ICGtesting.com
Printed in the USA
LVHW082135070819
626930LV00018B/846/P